37
THINGS
I WISH I'D
KNOWN
BEFORE MY
DIVORCE

LEARN HOW TO SAVE TIME, MONEY, YOUR KIDS, AND YOURSELF

NICOLE BARAS FEUER, M.S. &
FRANCINE BARAS, L.C.S.W.,
with LYNN PROWITT, M.A.

Original illustrations by Teresa Wojcicka

BALBOA.
PRESS
A DIVISION OF HAY HOUSE

Balboa Press books may be ordered through booksellers or by contacting:

Balboa Press
A Division of Hay House
1663 Liberty Drive
Bloomington, IN 47403
www.balboapress.com
1 (877) 407-4847

Printed in the United States of America.

ISBN: 978-1-4525-8944-2 (sc)
ISBN: 978-1-4525-8945-9 (e)

Library of Congress Control Number: 2014900062

Balboa Press rev. date: 04/24/2014

Contents

Notes on Using This Book

Fill out the "Important Contacts" list at the back of this book for quick access. Include people you'll frequently be in touch with throughout your divorce. Instead of searching for business cards floating around your desk drawer or phone numbers on post-it notes here and there, keep divorce-related contact info all in one spot to reduce aggravation. Also, in the appendixes, you'll find a collection of lists and forms that will come in handy. The back of the book has blank lined pages for making notes about things you want to remember. Take this book with you, literally and figuratively, as you travel through the days ahead.

Foreword

When I got married, I remember thinking that the ritual magically magnified everything that had already existed between us before— the wonderful and, yes, also the annoying. When I got divorced, that ritual seemed to magnify only the devastating and horrible.

By the time I finally filed for divorce, I had exhausted all other options and had twisted myself into a pretzel too many times trying everything possible to make the marriage work. What I finally discovered was that so much of my reasoning for not getting divorced was that I simply didn't know how, which for a high-achieving perfectionist was enough to keep me in an intolerable marriage. My fear of the unknown—and of not knowing—kept me stuck.

There is nothing I wouldn't have given at that time for this no-nonsense, to-the-point book you are holding in your hands. Nicole and Francine have created the exact companion I wish I'd had by my side as I cluelessly embarked on my journey through divorce. Perhaps then I wouldn't have hired the first lawyer I called, submissively endured a brutal mediation, deliriously agreed to pay maintenance to my ex-husband... the list goes on.

You are so lucky to have found this comprehensive guide. It's truly an invaluable treasure trove of information, resources, and actual tools that will carry you through the divorce process.

Let this book save you money and time. Let it support you, and even do some of the work for you, so that you can reserve your energy for restoration, rejuvenation, and a renewed lease on life.

—Nancy Levin, author of *Writing for My Life: Reclaiming the Lost Pieces of Me* and *Jump... And Your Life Will Appear*

Preface

We're lucky to live in a time where divorce carries far less stigma than it used to, and having a positive relationship with your ex is seen as hip and modern. When I faced my own divorce in 2009, I had been a divorce mediator for several years. I imagined, of course, that I'd have one of those relationships with my ex and a calm, uneventful divorce. It didn't go quite as I expected.

I married my high school sweetheart two years after I graduated college. In the first years of our marriage, we faced a series of obstacles that strained our relationship. We moved multiple times and ended up far from our families; he started a business, and we had infertility problems. Two years later we finally had our first son and two years after that our second. In the meantime, he was traveling all over the country, and to China at least four times a year for business. Tensions grew, we began fighting, and eventually we were miserable. But we loved our boys and were committed to keeping the family together.

Years later, I remember sitting in a mediation conference listening to a lecturer explain, with convincing research, that children who have regular access to both parents and whose parents have a peaceful divorce often do better in life than children who grow up exposed to yelling and tension in an intact family.

Like so many people, I believed divorce was bad for children, and like so many couples, my ex and I stayed married because we thought it was best for the kids, even as our marriage was unraveling. As I sat listening to that lecturer, I started asking myself, "Would my kids be better off with two parents who didn't fight but didn't live together? Is my marriage bad enough that my kids would actually benefit from a divorce?" These questions were so hard to answer that I pondered them for years.

After several years working as a divorce mediator, the one thing I could say for sure was that if I was going to get divorced, I would do it in a low-conflict way to minimize the effects on my kids. I would need to put aside the anger and learn to get along.

My ex and I talked a lot, and after seventeen years of marriage, we agreed getting divorced was the right decision. We were committed to doing everything possible to protect our boys from any negative effects. We told them together, and we began peacefully alternating our time with them.

Unfortunately, things quickly went from calm and rational to angry and high conflict. We fought over money, dividing our belongings, the kids, where we each would live, dating—you name it, we fought over it. I made rookie mistakes. We sent vicious texts back and forth, greatly escalating the conflict. Anxiety affected my memory and my ability to make decisions and focus. I was shocked at how overwhelmed I was and how much support I needed.

The breaking point was the day the police came to my house. My ex showed up to pick up the kids on a day I said wasn't his, and we let our anger get the better of us. We *both* called the police, and suddenly they were in the driveway.

Our sons were eight and ten at the time, and we looked at their faces and realized we had gone down the path we promised we never would. This was our rock-bottom and, fortunately, our turning point.

After that day we worked hard together to build a healthy and cooperative co-parenting relationship. In the pages of this book is all that I learned and wish I had known before we embarked on the journey of divorce.

I am happy to say my ex and I are now friends, are supportive of each other, communicate well about the kids, and are a calm and united front for our sons. I wish for you and your family an equally positive post-divorce life.

—Nicole Baras Feuer, MS

Introduction

Divorce just isn't what it used to be. The classic scenario in previous decades involved a devastating split, often preceded by a betrayal, leaving a stay-at-home mom reliant on alimony and child support to live and care for her kids. She kept primary custody, the dad took them to dinner Wednesday nights, and they packed bags to stay with him every other weekend. Divorce came with stigma and sadness, and the family unit essentially lost the father.

Most divorced families today look a lot different. In fact, there is no prevailing scenario anymore. More mothers have careers, more fathers are stay-at-home dads, and women and men often invest equal time parenting their children. Also, divorce is so common that it's become just one of dozens of transitions all of us may or may not face. As more people question the feasibility of humans "mating for life," getting a divorce is seen less as a "failure" and more as a sometimes necessary and even positive move forward.

Most people put a great deal of time and effort into finding a mate, creating a partnership, and making a marriage work. There's no reason not to put the same amount of energy into having a good divorce and post-divorce life. Nora Ephron once wrote this tagline for *The Huffington Post*'s section on divorce: "Marriages come and go, but divorce is forever." Don't let divorce derail your life: Start over smart.

This book will give you clear and succinct solutions whatever stage you're in. Maybe you haven't decided whether you want a divorce, or you're just a few steps into the process. Perhaps you're right in the thick of it or are working through post-divorce issues. This book is a simple guide—full of tips, lists, and how-tos—that will help you emotionally and practically. It is the result of countless hours of training, personal and professional experience, research, discussion, and collaboration. There's room for your own lists and notes, and it's designed to fit in your bag or briefcase. Carry it with you (and give a copy to your spouse/ex) while you navigate this sometimes painful and exasperating, sometimes hopeful and energizing, life transition.

PART 1

Should I Stay or Should I Go?

The tips in this section will help you feel confident that you've covered all your bases and gathered all the resources you need to make this sometimes very difficult decision. If you've already made your decision (or the decision was made for you), this information will set you up to feel more in control of the process and get you prepared for what's ahead.

1.

Have you tried everything?

Maybe you have done all you can. Maybe you've been hoping your spouse would change—and come to the difficult realization that it's not going to happen. The old truism applies. A person has to want to change, you can't make them. You can only change yourself.

Just make sure you'll never look back and say, "maybe we should have worked harder to save the marriage." To clearly assess whether or not your marriage is salvageable usually requires expert advice: marriage and family therapy, individual therapy, marital mediation (less "touchy feely" than therapy), or even a divorce coach or advisor. Don't call it quits until you can answer, "yes, I feel like we have tried everything we can."

2.
Take the driver's seat.

The fact that you are holding this book in your hands bodes well for your future. By driving, we mean taking control of the process and feeling empowered rather than helpless. Talk to people, listen to others' stories, and seek advice from experts (see #11). Learn about your state's divorce laws. Being well informed is your ticket to feeling competent and confident, which will help you make the best decisions for yourself and your family. As long as you're driving, you get to choose what direction you take at all the crossroads.

3.

Don't hang on for the wrong reasons.

Wrong reason #1: "It's scary; I don't want to give up my: house/money/lifestyle/in-laws/[fill in the blank]." It can take people five to ten years to progress from their first thought of getting a divorce to making the decision. But staying too long may allow anger and resentment to reach an unhealthy breaking point. Once there, it is much more difficult to have a good, low-conflict divorce and post-divorce relationship.

Wrong reason #2: "I want to stay for my kids, at least until they're out of the house." Keeping your kids in a dysfunctional household may not be better than having them weather a divorce. Even if your marriage is not rife with loud fighting but is instead rippled with quiet, chronic tension and anger, a miserable marriage is not good for kids. Keep in mind too that you may be so used to it that you don't notice the atmosphere you live in, but your kids most certainly do.

Ask yourself these questions:

- Is there regularly tension between you and your spouse?
- Do you and your spouse argue daily or almost daily?
- Do you sometimes feel rage toward your spouse?

- When was the last time your children saw you and your spouse hold hands, kiss, or put your arms around each other?
- Do you choose to do things together rather than separately, even when the kids aren't involved?
- Do you and your spouse ever laugh together?

Try to get out before you act out.

4.

If you've got even a smidgen of doubt, consider a trial separation.

Controlled separation—This approach is like a grown-up time-out for your marriage. It involves hiring a therapist to help you draw up a separation agreement that includes things like a time limit (e.g., three to six months); guidelines for contact (e.g., two phone calls per week); counseling sessions; rules regarding money, kids, visits; etc. The goal is to see if time apart while still working on the relationship can save the marriage. If it doesn't, the work that's been done can put you in a better starting place for the divorce process.

Legal separation—Not all states recognize legal separation. In those states that do, a legal separation can provide the structure and safety of a court-ordered contract (regarding finances, custody, etc.) without the finality of divorce.

Informal separation—Just as it sounds, this type of separation involves no formal agreement and no other parties besides you and your spouse. You'd be wise to get some guidelines and structure down in writing, but it's up to you. You should also check your state's laws regarding separation and when or if marital rights and obligations can change if you live apart. (See Sample Move-Out Agreement, appendix D.) Also, in some states you must live physically apart for a certain amount of time before you will be granted a divorce.

5.

Get support while you're deciding; don't agonize over the decision alone.

This may be the hardest and biggest decision you ever make. Even if you're typically a private person, reach out and get help and input from others. Don't get stuck in negative, cyclical thinking or become a hermit. Have honest talks with friends and family, but also seek out a neutral professional (such as a divorce advisor) and perhaps a support group to help you navigate the twists and turns and come to the best decisions.

6.

Organize your finances and get extra ink for your copier.

Whether or not you end up getting a divorce, being organized will reduce your stress and will likely decrease the number of billable hours you're charged by the professionals you may need to hire.

- Make a **list of your assets and liabilities**, everything you own that has a value or is a debt or obligation. The more info the better, but the most important thing is to have a complete list. (See appendix C.)
- Identify all **sources of income** you and your spouse have. (See Net Income Sheet, appendix B.)
- Make a **budget**. This will be a tremendous help when you have to prepare the standard financial statement or "affidavit," which is used for all financial reckoning in a divorce. (See Budget Form, appendix A.)
- **Record all account numbers**, PINs, important phone numbers, etc.
- **Make copies** of all your important documents—insurance policies, health benefit information, car registrations, membership cards, recent tax returns, investment account statements, titles/deeds, contracts, passports, wills, power of attorney, social security cards, etc.

- Make a **divorce file box.** We recommend that you take the time to create a file system for all the paperwork relevant to your divorce.
- **Clean up** as much of your marital debt as you can. Be aware: no matter what a divorce decree says, credit card companies can come after you if your name is on the account.
- Check your **personal credit score** using online services, or go to your local bank and ask how.
- If you don't have any **credit cards** in your name, get one or two and make at least the minimum payments on time to build up your personal credit history.
- If possible, make sure you always have some **cash in your own name** somewhere. Experts recommend having enough for three months of expenses put aside (including your house payment and other daily expenses).
- Know your whole **financial picture**, inside and out, now and what it would be post-divorce. If this process is overwhelming for you, seek out a certified divorce financial planner (CDFP) for help. This person can tell you what you need to do before you decide to divorce and how you can "afford" to get divorced. Start with the Association of Divorce Financial Planners at www.divorceandfinance.org.
- **De-clutter** your desk, office, and countertops. Start with these guidelines: Don't touch any piece of paper more than once; do something with it. Pick it up and toss it, file it, or act on it. With so much available online these days, you should end up with lean file folders and full recycling bins.

7.

Start making a plan before you do anything.

A clear and thoroughly considered plan is crucial to making a good decision. It will help you corral all the pros and cons and can help eliminate those "ugh, I didn't think of that" moments. Divorce affects every aspect of your life. American business magnate T. Boone Pickens said, "A fool with a plan can outsmart a genius with no plan." Your plan should answer these questions:

- What money will you use to pay an attorney's retainer and/ or any other professionals you need to hire for the divorce process? (See #11.)
- Will one of you need to get a job or return to work?
- Research your state's guidelines for determining child support. What can you expect in your situation? (Child support is based on spouses' incomes and other factors, and unlike alimony you can modify child support post-divorce.)
- Who will stay in the house and who will move out? Or could you live together until

you can afford to move apart? Is "bird-nesting" an option? (See #17.)

- Where does the spouse who leaves go?
- Is there enough income to support another house or apartment?
- Does the family pet stay, leave, or go back and forth with the kids?
- What will the parenting schedule be? Would you have sole or joint physical custody? Sole or joint legal custody? (Look up your own state's child custody laws so you understand your options.)
- Who keeps which car? Computer? Other valuable, shared equipment or tools?
- Who will pay the household bills? Consider everything: groceries, utilities, lawn care, emergency repairs or replacements (structural, heating/plumbing systems, appliances), etc.
- How will you share expenses? Will you send each other an itemized list at the end of each month? Will you exchange copies of receipts? Will you have a joint account for kids' expenses?

8.

If there's violence in your home, don't suffer in silence.

One out of every four women will be a victim of domestic violence in her lifetime, according to National Coalition Against Domestic Violence. It is one of the most chronically underreported crimes.

If you have experienced domestic violence, make a *safety plan*. Visit www.thehotline.org and look for "safety planning." Or call the twenty-four-hour hotline number: 1-800-799-SAFE. Also, the government's Office on Women's Health website lists domestic violence resources by state. Go to www.womenshealth.gov and look for "Violence Against Women."

Note: Most domestic violence websites have "quick escape" buttons at the top of their web pages, so you can leave the page instantly if needed.

"Breaking free of abuse is not simply a matter of walking out the door. Leaving is a process... On average, it takes seven attempts before an abused woman leaves her partner... The victim/survivor is the expert and the best judge of what she can and cannot do safely. So while a woman is deciding what the best course of action is, she needs to create a safety plan, which is a plan for staying as well as leaving."—From Domestic Violence Roundtable, an education and awareness group based in Massachusetts (www.domesticviolenceroundtable.org).

9

Look in the mirror and say, "I'd rather live alone in a teepee than spend another month with this person."

If you can say this with absolute conviction, you've probably made your decision.

PART 2

Okay, You're Getting a Divorce

This section is full of information and inspiration to get you through the sticky part—after the decision is made. It's time to end your marriage in the smartest, smoothest, most graceful way possible. These tips will help.

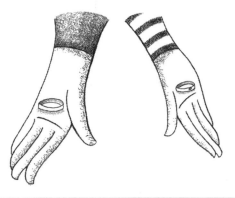

10.

Choose the divorce process that will work best for you.

Yes, you have options, and choosing the right one can make a huge difference in your finances and your emotional health. Whatever route you take, you'll fare better if you can work cooperatively with your spouse. Arguing costs money; in every type of divorce, the more you can resolve "outside the room," the less the divorce will cost. A high-conflict divorce takes a toll on more than your wallet; it can be very rough on kids. Whichever process you end up using, make it your goal to have a low-conflict divorce for the sake of your children. Here are the types of divorce and how they work:

1. *Mediation* (a cooperative divorce process)—You and your spouse hire an impartial mediator who works with both of you to resolve all your divorce issues, complete the required paperwork, and create an agreement that will form the basis for an uncontested divorce (one that doesn't require a judge to make any decisions for you). Mediation allows for more creative solutions than does a traditional, attorney-centered divorce. A good mediator (who may or may not be an attorney, see #11) helps spouses work together to create an agreement both can live with. Your mediator will likely teach communication and problem-solving skills along the way that will be useful in your future dealings with each other. For this process to be effective, you and

your spouse must be committed to working together to create an agreement without relying on the court system. Mediators have to remain neutral, so you should hire your own attorney to advise you as you go and to review the final divorce agreement in the context of your interests and rights. This attorney must be mediator-friendly, which means they support the process of mediation. Mediation may still end up being your least expensive option because only one professional handles the process from start to finish.

2. *Collaborative* (a cooperative divorce process)—Both parties hire their own lawyers, specially trained in collaborative family law. The process may also involve a financial expert (such as a CDFP, see #11) and a collaboratively trained mental health provider and/or other professionals. This team then helps the couple negotiate based on what they need, rather than just on their legal rights, and works toward emotional healing too. All parties involved pledge in writing to resolve the issues without the involvement of the court. If the team doesn't succeed in reaching an agreement or one of the spouses wants to end the process and go to court, the team has to be disbanded and new lawyers must be hired.

3. *Litigation* (an adversarial divorce process)—You and your spouse retain (hire) your own lawyers to represent you throughout the divorce process. One spouse has to be the plaintiff and one the defendant. (This is a formality left over from the days when a couple couldn't get a divorce without showing cause or fault, and one spouse had to "sue" the other one for divorce.) You meet with your lawyers separately and they prepare your case, communicate with each other and the court, and prepare all the paperwork to take your case through to settlement or trial. Even though only 1 percent of divorce cases actually go to trial, litigation attorneys

must prepare your case as if it could. Because litigation is set up to be an adversarial process, this can make it lengthy, costly and emotionally difficult for all involved, particularly children.

4. *Do-it-yourself*—You fill out and file all the necessary court documents yourself. This option is best in cases where the spouses are in complete agreement about property division, custody and financial support, and when assets and debt information is simple and straightforward. You may still hire a mediator, accountant, document preparation service, or other experts to help in areas where there is disagreement or complicated material involved.

5. *Arbitration*—The divorcing couple and their respective attorneys choose and agree on an arbitrator, usually a retired family court judge or a very senior divorce attorney. The arbitrator is presented with the specific issues that are in dispute. After a hearing, the arbitrator renders a decision, called an "award," on the disputed issues. In most cases, this decision is binding. Divorce arbitration can be used in place of a court trial in a traditional, adversarial divorce. Or, it may be used in a collaborative or mediated divorce when an impasse has occurred.

11.

Recruit your team of professionals.

If you thought all you needed was a lawyer or mediator, we want to change your mind. For one thing, the more specific and varied expertise you bring onboard, the more smoothly your divorce ship will sail. Second, relying on other experts rather than having an attorney handle everything can often save you money. Get referrals from trusted, professional sources, not only from friends and acquaintances. (See #15.)

Depending on your individual situation, your divorce team might include any or all of the following:

- **Certified divorce financial analyst or planner (CDFA or CDFP)**—A financial expert who can explain child support, and maintenance and property division as it applies to your situation. They can advocate for your needs with your attorney and create strategies for your settlement. In addition, they can help you plan for financial independence and security.
- **Divorce advisor/coach**—A divorce expert who may be a lawyer or have other professional training in areas such as finance or mental health. The person may have specific training and certification. These divorce professionals will likely charge hourly and can guide you through the phases of your divorce—helping with everything from organizing paperwork and managing stress to reentering the workforce.

- **Therapist**—Someone with formal mental health training (a psychiatrist, psychologist, or licensed clinical social worker), preferably with a specialty in families and children and experience working with families of divorce.
- **Parenting coordinator**—Often an attorney with additional, specialized training, who helps parents resolve disputes and improve their co-parenting skills. This can save parties the expense and hassle of going back to court.
- **Divorce mediator**—A specially trained, neutral professional, typically an attorney or a mental health professional, who meets with both spouses to work together on a divorce agreement. (See #10.)
- **Attorney**—Someone trained in family or matrimonial law who you will likely need, depending on the type of divorce you choose, at some point in the process. This person might serve as a review attorney, a collaborative law attorney, or a litigator.

You may want to consider hiring other professionals who can help you with matters related to your divorce—for their specialized expertise and to reduce money spent on your mediator and/or attorney. These others might include any of the following:

- **Tax accountant**—An accountant with tax expertise who prepares tax returns.
- **Forensic accountant**—An accountant who specializes in finding hidden assets (if you suspect your spouse may be hiding money); their fees are typically quite high.
- **Pension/retirement planning advisor**—If you have a CDFA or CDFP, you may not need this. But be sure someone on your team thoroughly researches all pensions, IRAs, 401(k)s, etc., and helps you understand the implications for a QDRO (a legal document that dictates how retirement funds are divided up in a divorce).
- **Wealth management expert**—A financial advisor with expertise in investing and money management, often from

a large financial-services company, with resources that extend to tax advice and estate planning.

- **Insurance expert** (health, life, home, car, renters, umbrella, etc.)—Whether it's an insurance specialist or another financial expert, make sure to have someone on your team who can explain and help you navigate COBRA, the provision that allows a person to remain covered by a spouse's health insurance for a certain period after a divorce.
- **Credit/debt counselor**—A person trained to help others manage debt and credit problems.
- **Career counselor**—A person trained in helping people start new careers, change careers, or return to a previous career.
- **Employment agent**—Depending on your skill set and how quickly you need to find a job, going to an agency may be the easiest and fastest way to a paycheck.
- **Real estate agent**—A trusted Realtor can help you determine the value of your home, what you can afford, and what you can expect to find on the market.
- **Guardian ad litem**—A guardian appointed to represent the interests of the children, usually an attorney.

12.
Keep calm (and carry on).

As you juggle all the moving parts in your life during a divorce, you need to make every effort to decrease your stress.

Why? Not only does stress wreak havoc on your physical health, research has shown that it can interfere with brain function, including memory and learning. To make the best decisions for yourself and your children throughout the divorce process, it's crucial that you use all the resources you have to keep calm and yes, carry on.

The following are some proven methods for lowering stress and ameliorating its effects on your health. No one technique is right for everyone, and practicing them in combination is your best bet.

Another tip: With many of these techniques, practice makes perfect. Don't be discouraged if you don't see immediate results; you'll get more noticeable relief as you become adept. Of course if nothing seems to help and your anxiety is interfering with your ability to function, see a mental health professional.

✓ **Exercise.** You've heard it before: Exercise is like a miracle drug. It improves physical health, mental health, and cognitive function. It also has an established and powerful ability to reduce stress and mitigate the effects of stress on your body.

✓ **Meditation (mindfulness).** Mindfulness meditation is a technique so simple you can learn how to do it just by reading about it on the Internet. You're better off getting a book or audiotape, but either way it's worth the effort. Studies have shown just minutes a day to be effective for chronic pain, depression, and stress.

✓ **Massage therapy** can lower blood pressure—and keep it lower for days after, according to some research. Don't think of it as a luxury; it's preventive health care. Tip: When time or money is short, there's always the fifteen-minute chair massage.

✓ **Breathing exercises.** What do exercise, yoga, and meditation have in common? They alter your natural breathing pattern. When time is short, have a go-to breathing exercise you can use to calm yourself. Google "breathing exercises" or just close your eyes and count ten slow, even breaths through your nose. Works like magic.

✓ **Muscle-relaxation techniques.** Progressively relaxing your body from top to bottom, one muscle group at a time, has been effective in treating stress-related disorders—and it's a great technique for getting yourself to sleep.

✓ **Writing in a journal or diary.** Research suggests that it's important not to just "vent" negative emotions when journaling, as that can cause backlash and make you feel worse. Instead, focus on understanding and trying to make sense of stressful or painful situations and events.

✓ **Cognitive behavioral therapy (CBT)** is one of the most common psychotherapy techniques used today. It's usually more interactive than traditional psychotherapy, and you may only attend a limited number of sessions. The therapist typically teaches techniques to help you change negative thought patterns.

13.

Tell the kids, together (but not until you read this!)

It's important to tell your children as soon as possible once you've reached a decision. Delaying leaves the "elephant in the room." Whether or not they show it, they'll know something is up and may be stressed. Customize the guidelines below according to your kids' ages. (See #14 for kids' reactions to divorce by age and stage.)

With a mixed-age group of children, speak at the level of the youngest child. Tell the older ones they can ask any questions they have after, when the little ones are elsewhere.

With kids three and younger, simply tell them, "Mommy/Daddy is moving to a new place." Keep it very simple—where she or he is going, and when she or he is coming back next.

Here are excellent guidelines for children ages four and older:

1. Plan what you're going to say and when. It's important that you present a united front.
2. Make sure all immediate family members are present, including both parents.
3. Give a simple explanation for the divorce, but be as honest and straightforward as you can.

- Don't lie. If they sense it or find out the truth, you will lose their trust and confidence. They may think, *What else are they lying about?*
- On the other hand, don't give more detail than they need or can handle. Don't tell them, "Mom cheated" or "Dad lost all our money."

4. Do not assign blame. Present a united front and decisions as mutual. You're their parents forever, and they need to be able to love and respect both of you and have good relationships with both of you.

5. Emphasize that they are in no way responsible for the divorce, that it's something between Mom and Dad.
   - It may seem odd and counterintuitive to parents, but one thing that divorce experts have found to be overwhelmingly true is that children of all ages and types tend to blame themselves for their parents' divorce.

6. Tell them clearly that there is nothing they could possibly do to change it—that the divorce is happening and it can't be undone.
   - Partly because kids tend to blame themselves, they often take it upon themselves to fix things by being extra good or, conversely, acting out and causing problems. They may truly believe they have the power to bring you back together.

7. Emphasize that both parents will continue to love and take care of them.

8. Tell them everything you can think of that you know will stay the same: their house (if one of you is staying), their school, their friends, and their activities. Also, let them know what traditions will remain the same, such as Easter at Grandma's, the annual summer lake trip, etc.

9. Tell them what will likely or definitely change (e.g., they will spend part of their time in a new house with Mom or Dad and go back and forth, they'll split holidays, etc).

10. Acknowledge their feelings. Tell them it's okay to feel whatever they're feeling—sad, angry, worried, or even nothing at all, just numb.

11. Encourage them to ask questions and express themselves. And watch your own reactions to what they say. You don't want them to wish they'd never spoken up. Also, let them know it's all right to talk to other trusted adults—at school, at church, to family friends, etc. Tell them your divorce is not a secret and that it's a common family transition, nothing to be embarrassed about.

14.

Understand your child's developmental stage and reactions to divorce.

Divorce is usually a stressful experience for children, regardless of age. At first, children are likely to feel vulnerable and powerless and will grieve the loss of their intact family. Those feelings may come with anger or withdrawal. Remember that kids are generally adaptable and resilient (much more so than we are), and if you're committed to keeping divorce conflict to a minimum and to co-parenting in a cooperative and friendly spirit with your ex, your kids will be okay.

Here are some guidelines that may help you understand children's reactions and the best ways to support them, by age group:

3 to 5 years old (preschoolers): At this stage, children can't understand the concept of divorce. They may still confuse reality and fantasy and believe in dreams and wishes coming true. They may think the divorce is about them, something they have done, and may worry both parents might abandon them. If you notice regressive behaviors (bedwetting, sleep issues, etc.), have patience and understand these are likely temporary. (Seek professional help if they persist.) Read age-appropriate books on divorce with them and help them verbalize feelings they may not have the words for.

Give loads of affection and reassurances that they are loved and protected and that they will always have both their parents.

5 to 11 years old (elementary school): From five to seven, children still have very basic thinking skills. They may be afraid their parents will abandon them or get angry and no longer want them. Seven- to eight-year-olds are in the developmental stage where family and a sense of belonging is paramount. It's common for kids this age to fantasize about where they came from and wonder if they were adopted. Maintain as many family activities as possible—such as grandparent visits, family dinners, and special family outings. Try to give them plenty of structure and routine and set up a predictable parenting schedule.

12 to 15 years old (early adolescence): This stage usually marks the onset of anxiety about identity ("Who am I?" "What am I like?") and separation issues (torn between independence and attachment to parents). Kids this age may respond to a divorce with depression, acting out sexually, and/or having trouble at school. Although they may seem more interested in their peers, they're still attuned to what's happening in the family. They will be particularly aware of parents' behavior around sexuality and dating, when and if that begins. Keep lines of communication open with them by staying neutral on topics related to the divorce. Allow them to react and share thoughts and feelings without being judged, and encourage and help them maintain access to both parents.

15 to 18 years old (late adolescence): Older adolescents are preparing for their own separation from the family and may talk with and rely more on their peers. Teachers and other role models may also be important. Although more independent, kids in this age group will still need your guidance and to stay involved with the family. Teens can develop depression, anger, and loneliness and may act out sexually or with drugs and alcohol. Keep them talking and sharing feelings by providing nonjudgmental communication. Allow them some say in their schedule, showing respect for their social and school activities. Make it easy for them to talk to trusted adults outside the family. But make sure they feel secure in the knowledge that you are still their parent and in charge.

Note: Inform staff at your child's school about what's happening at home. Ask about school resources, such as a social worker or psychologist and "changing family" or "banana splits" support groups. Also, be sure to tell the other adults in your child's life: dance teachers, sports coaches, etc. The last thing you want is an unknowing coach getting tough and yelling at your kid the day after your spouse moves out. Also, mention your situation to your pediatrician at the next appointment.

15.

Be smart about finding a lawyer or mediator.

1. Gather recommendations from friends and professionals you trust (such as a divorce advisor, financial advisor, doctor, therapist, lawyer, etc.). They will likely be able to refer you to a credible divorce attorney or mediator.

2. When someone gives you names, go online and research them (and their firm, if they have one). Find out how long they have been in practice, how they market themselves, and what they specialize in. For a mediator, you may want to visit www.mediate.com. For lawyers, a good place to start is the American Academy of Matrimonial Lawyers: www.aaml.org.

3. Next, call. You'll get a sense of how easy or difficult it is to get them on the phone, and you can ask about their fees. Mediators typically charge by the hour. Lawyers usually charge an advance (called a retainer) and have an hourly fee. If the retainer alone is way out of your budget, cross them off your list and ask if they can recommend someone more junior perhaps, with lower fees.

4. Set up meetings and interview everyone still on your list. They should not charge you for the initial consultation.

5. Go to these meetings prepared with questions and with a practiced, concise, objective summary of your situation. Be sure to ask them to explain their approach, and with lawyers, ask who handles the day-to-day work. If they delegate a lot of the

work to a junior associate, ask to meet that person too. Other questions to ask:

- (lawyer) Do you practice only matrimonial law or other types of law also?
- What is your typical mix of clients?
- How busy are you? Do you have plenty of time for my case?
- Do you usually bring in other divorce professionals? Who are they? What do they charge for their time?
- (lawyer) Do you ever work on mediated divorce cases or collaborative cases?
- (mediator) About what percentage of your cases end in stalemate and the parties have hired lawyers?
- (lawyer) How often do you go to court?
- (lawyer) How often do those cases go to trial?
- How much money does a typical client end up spending?

Take notes. Then go home and let the meeting sink in for a while. Don't make a decision on the spot. Your lawyer has to be someone with whom you feel comfortable and trust, as he or she will likely be with you through some tough times. Follow your intuition. A final word: Whenever possible, bring a friend along to meetings in which a lot of information will be discussed. It's enormously helpful to have a second set of ears and someone who can take notes for you.

16.

If you have to keep living together, create rules for doing so until you can move apart.

- Implement your parenting plan as if you were living separately, or agree on other, clear arrangements about parenting time. Put it in writing. (See #19 and #26.)
- Agree on sleeping arrangements. Will you have separate rooms, and do these rooms have locks for privacy?
- Agree on computer/tablet use. Will you have separate computers and/or will you share a computer and need separate, password-protected logins?
- Agree on bathroom use. Use separate bathrooms, if possible, or establish showering times and perhaps some rules relating to etiquette.
- Agree to let each other have private lives. Neither of you should question the other's comings and goings except as it relates to the parenting plan.
- Make a plan for household chores, such as pet feeding, laundry, dishes, and cleaning.
- Agree on a plan for food and meals.

- Agree on rules about houseguests and, if appropriate, dating. (See #33.)
- Agree not to argue in front of the kids. If possible, schedule weekly times to talk away from the children.
- Agree to use e-mail or text messaging, etc., for communicating about the children, the schedule, and divorce matters to keep the children's exposure and stress to a minimum.

17.
Don't move out in a huff.

When it comes time for you or your spouse to move out of the family home, do this with some forethought.

- If your situation allows, find a place that is close to where your ex is living. You'll see things get left behind, and if you don't live close, it can be an ordeal—for them and for you—when they have to retrieve something from the other house. Also, it may be good to have your ex nearby when there's an emergency or you need last-minute coverage. Kids benefit in other ways too, from having both their houses in the same general area; it's easier to make and maintain friendships, possibly take the same school bus, and be in the same proximity to their activities for carpooling, etc.
- Create a written agreement that ensures that the spouse moving out will not constitute "abandonment," and he or she won't lose any of his or her rights to the house, marital assets, or children. You should discuss this type of agreement with a lawyer before you sign. (See Sample Move-Out Agreement, appendix D.)
- Have a parenting agreement in place before the move. (See #19.)
- Inventory the marital property, with lists and photos of anything very valuable (either in price or sentimental value).
- If a second home large enough for kids is too much of a financial strain, consider "bird-nesting." This means the

35

kids stay in the family home and the parents come and go, according to the parenting schedule. The financial benefit is that you and your spouse can share an inexpensive studio apartment or stay with family or friends during the other's parenting time.

- Some states require that you live separately for a certain amount of time before you can be granted a divorce. Check your state's requirements.

18.

Make a new nest.

If you are moving to a new place, take the time and care to create a comfortable and inviting space. You don't want your kids eating off cardboard boxes and sleeping in a room with bare walls. It's not good for you either. Make it homey. Let the kids choose something from their bedrooms to bring to the new place. Take them on a weekend excursion to a flea market or tag sale, and pick out some fun things together. If they're old enough, let your kids pick out decorative keys at the hardware store and have house keys made for them.

19.
Be a detail freak with your parenting plan.

Kids need both parents. No matter what you think of your ex, research shows that children do best when they have both parents in their lives. It sounds obvious, but when you create this plan, remember to put the kids first—before your own anger, frustration, or fears. The more you can cooperate and compromise with your ex, the better your children will fare.

Take your time and work out as detailed a parenting plan as you can; don't just wing it. Ideally, you and your ex will be amicable and flexible, and the exhaustive detail you include won't end up being necessary. But it's an insurance policy that may save you a lot of grief when a conflict arises.

Here are some important questions your parenting plan should answer:

1. **Weekly schedule:** What days and nights do the children spend with each parent? Where and how will they be picked up or dropped off? How do those details change during summer and school vacations, snow days, holidays, early dismissals, delayed openings, sick days, etc.? Which parent should the school nurse call when a child is sick?

2. **Yearly schedule:** How will you share holidays? (See Holidays and Vacations Scheduling Chart, appendix G.) Be specific about times. For example, if a parent has the kids for Christmas, does that mean from noon Christmas Eve to noon Christmas Day? Also, don't use vague terms like

"the Thanksgiving holiday." Address Thanksgiving Day, the Friday after, and the weekend.

3. **Communication:** What are the guidelines for the parents' communication? E-mail only except in emergency? Do you want to have a rule about response time? Limit correspondence content to facts only—and no judging, criticizing, or using sarcastic or inflammatory words. (See #28.)

4. **Communication with kids:** What are your guidelines for phone communication with the children? (A set daily time for phone contact can prevent problems and resentment, and most importantly take the burden off the kids.) Will you agree to give the children privacy when on the phone with their other parent?

6. **First right of refusal:** When one of you cannot care for your kids during your custody time, will you agree on giving the other parent "first right of refusal" before making arrangements for another adult to stay with them? If it's just for a couple of hours, or only if it's for more than X hours? Or only if it's overnight? Consider times when you're out for an evening (perhaps on a date), gone for the day to an event, or for a longer period such as on a business trip. Think also about one of you getting a bad flu or breaking an ankle, etc.

7. **Extracurricular activities:** Who handles choices/ decisions, sign-up, payment, and transportation, and what happens when activities fall on the other parent's days?

8. **Medical/mental health:** Who handles appointments? Does the scheduling parent need to have an agreement from the other parent, or is notification enough? Who pays for which appointments/treatments and how?

9. **Travel:** For what type of travel (out of town, out of state, or out of country) is permission/notification of the other parent required? How much advance notice will you require? You may need a notarized "affidavit of parental consent" form. (See appendix H.)

10. **Education:** Does one parent have decision-making power over the other in matters of schooling, or is agreement required? What is the plan for financing college and/or other advanced education? (If your kids are very young and college seems too far away, you may want to leave this to be decided at a later date.)

11. **Religion:** Are any rules or agreements required around the children's religious upbringing?

12. **Kids' vital documents:** Who will keep the originals? Will the other parent keep copies?

13. **Major disagreements:** What is the protocol when/if there's an impasse regarding parenting issues? (If possible, assign a mediator, parenting coordinator, therapist, guardian ad litem, etc., that you both agree on, to be your go-to for parenting plan conflicts.)

14. **Special days:** What days do you want to ensure that you see your kids (for example your birthday, the first day of school, graduation days, when there's a recital, bat/bar mitzvahs, etc.)?

15. **Special occasions:** How do you want to handle times when relatives or special friends are visiting and the children are with the other parent? Or special events like weddings, big birthdays, anniversaries, etc.?

16. **Vacation time limits:** How long will you allow each other to take the children for vacation? And will you set limits as to how those days fall into the schedule so that one parent doesn't go more than a certain amount of time without seeing the children?

17. **Relocating:** Think carefully about the possibility of one of you wanting or needing to move. Can you both agree to stay within certain geographical limits until the children graduate high school?

20.

Stay away from the crazy divorce people (and don't become one).

You know them. Divorce can be ugly and a source of long-lasting anger, bitterness, frustration, and despair. Some people are stuck in the muck and cannot help but regale you with their tales of betrayal and angst ("Oh my god, have I told you what he did last week?"). You don't want to end up caught in a grocery store parking lot with one of these folks, topping each other's divorce stories. While you are in the midst of this life transition, surround yourself with positive people who help you look forward and focus on what's good. Try your hardest to forgive (see #23), accept, and look forward, not back.

21.

Love your children more than you hate your ex.

While it may seem obvious, remind yourself of this every day. Your children need you to not get stuck in anger and negativity. (And of course you shouldn't "hate" your ex or anyone for that matter, but you get the idea.)

22.
Take the high road, always.

Divorce isn't always "fair" and if you keep in mind that maintaining your personal integrity is more important than being right or winning, you will make better choices and create more positive outcomes. Modeling maturity and kindness above all else is one of the very best gifts you can give your children.

Anytime you're about to see or speak to your ex, ask yourself, "How would my kids like to see me behave right now? What would make them most comfortable?" In other words, make choices that keep tension and negative feelings at bay.

PART 3

After the Divorce Dust Settles

If you have children, you are forever connected to your ex. Your post-divorce struggles may be less intense, but the practical, everyday communicating about kid-related matters never ends. Heed the advice that follows to ensure a peaceful future for you, your ex, and your children.

23.

Practice forgiveness: it's never too late to bury the hatchet.

Have you ever heard the adage, "Anger is like drinking poison and waiting for the other person to die"? The one who gets sick is the person fuming with anger day in and day out. This is more than a metaphor.

Reasons people find it so hard to forgive:

1) They think it somehow excuses or condones the other's behavior, that it "lets the jerk off the hook," and that justice should be served before forgiveness.
2) Being angry can feel powerful, and that can be hard to give up. When someone is angry and venting, you may notice he or she is animated, energized, and articulate. When chronicling the highlights of his or her divorce story, he or she lines up the transgressions of the ex like a trial lawyer. Now imagine that person letting go of the anger and simply forgiving. The powerful feeling is gone, and there's no more thrill in telling the story.
3) Being angry is easier than feeling the feeling beneath it, which is most often fear.

"Forgiveness is really a choice we make," writes psychologist Paula Bloom. "If we wait for the feeling to fill our hearts, inspiring us to forgive, we could spend our lives waiting. It is a decision—a conscious decision. While we don't have control over events that occurred in the past, we have some say over what role those events play in our present" (from "This Emotional Life," PBS blogs: http://www.pbs.org/thisemotionallife/blogs/ toxic-and-intoxicating-effects-resentment).

Why forgive? The scientific research on forgiveness is impressive. The ability to forgive is associated with better health— for example, lower blood pressure, less depression, and improved immune system and cardiovascular function. And, of course, it's the antidote to that poisonous anger you've been "drinking." Forgiving makes you feel better from the inside out.

24.

You're free of being wed in matrimony; don't be bound forever in acrimony.

"It's as if my ex doesn't *want* to get along." Does that ring a bell? Some people, usually without realizing it, keep the fighting going just to stay connected. The arguing and tension, though negative, is emotional and maintains a bond with your ex.

If you think your ex is being antagonistic just to stay connected to you, we recommend you disengage. If you engage, you'll only perpetuate the acrimony. If you don't, then a new, positive connection may develop between you. A useful strategy: Respond simply with, "I'm not going to argue with you."

Psychotherapist Howard Yahm wrote in his article "Divorce-Induced Emotions and the Healing Paradigm:" "When being married in affection turns into being divorced in anger, the couple is often more attached and involved with each other in hate than they ever were in love" (www.divorcemediation.com).

Anger is addictive. (See #23.) Here are some tips to help you deal with angry feelings and habits:

- As tempting as it may be to criticize and complain about your ex, don't. You share children; you will always be connected to this person.

- Even if your ex did horrible things, you need to stop reliving them. Instead, leave them in the past, live in your present, and think positively about your future.
- Limit who you talk to about your ex and your divorce issues or you might be sorry later. You don't want your "dirty laundry" strewn around your community because, one way or another, it will come back to your kids.
- Beware of venting, trying to convince others how bad your ex is, and becoming frustrated when they don't share your indignation.
- Learn to be less rigid and more accepting of your ex and his or her parenting, lifestyle choices, etc. There isn't one "right" way to raise children, and kids can adapt very well to two different households and parenting styles.

And of course, if you find yourself unable to move past your anger, get help from a professional.

25.

Nobody said this was going to be easy.

Of course you should be prepared for some bumps in the road. Some you might encounter:

- The characteristics and behaviors of your ex that you found difficult when you were married won't just magically disappear. They may never go away and will likely become magnified and harder to tolerate.
- Ideally, you and your ex will compromise and work together well as co-parents, but you may have to do a significant amount of "letting go" in parenting matters. You'll only have control over what happens in your house. You may have little or no say over what your kids eat, watch, wear, hear, and do at your ex's house.
- You may face unexpected reactions and behavior from friends, in-laws, colleagues, and neighbors. Some people are uncomfortable with divorce, and some friends may pull away. (But there will also be those who sympathize and are proud of you.)
- You may feel deep sadness, even if you were the one to ask for the divorce. This is normal grief. Give yourself time to mourn the loss of your marriage.

Don't be discouraged or start blaming yourself. It's part of the process, and you can't control everything. Divorce is a kind of death, and you should expect to go through some version of the five stages of grief: denial, anger, bargaining, depression, and acceptance. You may experience one, some, or all of these "stages," and they can occur in any order and also overlap.

1. Denial—"I'm fine. Everything's fine, really."
2. Anger—"This is so unfair! Why is this happening to me?"
3. Bargaining—"I'll do anything you want. I'll quit drinking/ smoking/cheating."
4. Depression—"What's the point? I have nothing left. I don't even care anymore."
5. Acceptance—"Things are going to be okay. We'll all survive."

Give yourself a break, and ask yourself, "Am I doing the best I can right now?" You probably are, so cut yourself some slack and keep your chin up. Go back to the mirror and say, "I will get through this and thrive in my new life."

26.

Follow the golden rules of co-parenting (and share them with your ex).

After you memorize the rules below (we're not kidding), go to the back of the book and check out the Children's Bill of Rights, appendix E. It wouldn't be a bad idea to memorize those too. If your ex isn't able to follow these rules right now, follow them yourself and model how it should be done. You may be surprised to find that your ex will follow your lead.

1. Don't let them hear you badmouthing your ex.

When you bash your ex, it's almost like you're telling your kids you don't like certain parts of them. They internalize your words, and they know full well they have this other person's genes. Also, the person you're criticizing is someone they love no matter what. Hearing you say negative things about that person hurts and can make them worry that you'll stop loving them too. Keep in mind that kids will grow up and form their own opinions. If you badmouth, there's a good chance, whether you're right or wrong, that they'll "shoot the messenger" and resent you.

2. **Your kids are not reporters. Do not quiz them about your ex or their life at the other house, and don't communicate through them.**

    Don't ask your kids a lot of questions when they're at the other parent's house or when they first come back to you after a weekend away. Instead, make leading statements that keep conversations light and on neutral subjects and allow kids to relax and mention things they want to bring up. (On the phone: "Right now, the dog is at the window trying desperately to catch a fly with her mouth. Ha! What's up with you, sweetie?" On first seeing them after a weekend away: "I love that shirt on you; it brings out the color of your eyes.")

    Once conversation is rolling, don't ask questions that put your kids on the spot. For example, avoid the temptation to ask them how old their father's girlfriend is. Even seemingly innocent questions like, "What did you do last night?" "What did you eat for dinner?" or "Who was there?" can be subtly loaded. Your kids can sense when you react negatively and feel like they're betraying the other parent while maybe also upsetting you.

3. **Never put your children in the middle of an argument or make them choose one parent over the other.**

    Don't make the mistake of thinking you're giving them freedom or just "being flexible" by asking which parent they'd like to drive with to a game or which house they'd like to stay in when there's a scheduling ambiguity, or even who they'd like to sit next to at an event. Whether or not they show it, making them choose one of you puts a burden on them they shouldn't have to shoulder. You and your ex need to tell your children who they're going with and when and where to sit. (And whenever you can, take the high road: "Go sit with your dad; you haven't seen him in a while").

4. **Don't let them hear you talk about money matters that relate to the divorce.**

    For one, until they're adults themselves and managing their own money and bills, they cannot truly make sense of these things and are likely to misunderstand. Second, money can be a tricky issue with lots of power and emotion attached. It's best to keep those matters completely "off their plate."

5. Don't compromise their time with the other parent.

If something fun is happening that they will miss because they are not with you, don't tell them about it or at least not until after the fact. If it's something significant, like a rare chance to see a special relative who's in town, go to your ex and ask if you can alter the schedule *before* saying anything to your kids. Also, when the kids are with your ex, resist telling them about the exciting and wonderful things that will happen as soon as they return to you. Do everything you can to help ensure that they can be equally happy in *both* houses.

27.

If you can't co-parent, parallel parent.

Good co-parenting is low-conflict: You and your ex talk about your children's needs in a healthy way; you agree on parenting values; you have consistent parenting styles and few arguments about your children; you never put your kids in the middle; and you solve differences peacefully. (See #26.) Children of divorce fare best when their parents have a cooperative relationship and can communicate about the kids and interact without antagonism.

However, if parents can't cooperate much of the time, and hostility and conflict reign, the best strategy may be *parallel parenting*. Whether or not kids are exposed to parental conflict is the single-most important factor in how well they adjust to divorce.

Like "parallel play," a term used to describe how toddlers play alongside each other before they develop the skills for interacting, parallel parenting describes a way for parents to take care of their children with a minimum amount of direct interaction. The goal should be to work toward a time when, just as toddlers eventually learn to play together, you and/or your ex are no longer angry and can co-parent cooperatively.

Some ideas for parallel parenting:

- Limit interaction to the exchange of important information. For example, you need to tell your ex if you gave your child Tylenol for a headache two hours ago (so he or she doesn't give the child more too soon). You do not need to tell your ex that you took the kids to the mall or give advice on what your ex should do with the kids next weekend.

- Keep fighting the urge to engage with your ex until it becomes routine. Don't respond to criticism, and don't mention when your ex is late or lets the kids drink soda or forgets to bring something. And do not use sarcasm.
- Create a routine for non-urgent communication, such as an e-mail exchange once a week or twice a month, etc.
- Use e-mail as your sole method of non-emergency communication, so you have time to compose your words carefully and edit out anything emotional, inflammatory, sarcastic, etc. Make sure every sentence contains only necessary information. E-mail is also useful as an informational record you can turn back to if needed.
- Agree to make copies of anything you receive pertaining to a child—team rosters, report cards, test results, appointment reminders, etc.—and send to each other as soon as possible.
- Divvy up or take turns being responsible for haircuts, medical and dental appointments, back-to-school shopping, etc. Be reasonable and clear to avoid any possible conflicts.
- Agree to make your own connections to all of your children's teachers, coaches, friends, etc., so that one parent doesn't have to keep the other in the loop.
- If your children are very young or have special issues, agree to writing a "transition-day memo" each week so the receiving parent can be made aware of what's been going on (latest eating or sleeping details, medications, emotions, etc.)
- Have an agreed-upon neutral forum (a parenting coordinator, mediator, therapist, etc.) in place to help handle any parenting impasses that may occur.

28.

Abide by these communication dos and don'ts.

DO:

- When you're angry about something, **write an e-mail** in which you vent all your frustrations, but don't send it. Then walk away. Come back later to write the real e-mail after you've cooled down. Leave out anything unkind, inflammatory, or sarcastic. Don't kid yourself; sending an angry e-mail will always make things worse.
- Think of and speak to your ex as though he or she is **a business associate** (so you focus on the issue at hand, not the emotions).
- When you are on the phone (or in person), **speak slowly** and keep these phrases handy for any conversations that may be confrontational:
  "I need to think about that. I'll have to get back to you."
  "I'm sorry, I'm in the middle of something. Can I get back to you?"
  "I understand. Hmmm."
  "I hear what you're saying."
- **Say or do something kind** whenever the opportunity comes along. Small kindnesses can yield big rewards. For example, text your ex a picture of your kids when they're with you, or ask the kids to call or text your ex to tell them

about something fun or special, allowing him or her to feel included in the kids' day or experience. You will love it when your ex returns the favor.

DON'T:

- **Bring up past disagreements** or transgressions. Look forward, not back, or things will go off track.
- Get caught up in **tit for tat** ("You were twenty minutes late, so I am keeping them twenty minutes longer on Sunday..." "You never had him call me after his soccer game, so why should I have him call you?"). Take the high road.
- **Sweat the small stuff** ("You took them for ice cream on the way to my house? I have dinner in the oven!" "She's wearing the same clothes I dressed her in two days ago!"). Take a deep breath and ask yourself, *Is this really a big deal?* Pick your battles.

29.
Don't coddle; empower your children.

Divorced parents tend to sometimes make more lenient or indulgent parenting decisions because they feel:

a. guilty that their "failure" has resulted in the children feeling upset or dislodged, having to live in two places and regularly separate from one parent or the other;

b. overly celebratory when they're with the kids because they've missed them so much;

c. in competition with the other parent, wanting the kids to enjoy and be happy (perhaps happier) during their parenting time;

d. afraid that they might "ruin" their first day back together or last day before they leave by nagging and disciplining them, even though appropriate; or

e. all of the above.

When you catch yourself behaving this way, remember that your primary goal is for your kids to emerge from this divorce—and from their childhood—with the confidence and skills they need to go out into the world and forge a happy, successful life. Guess what doesn't move them toward this end: Giving them too many things, not setting boundaries for them, doing too much for them, disciplining inconsistently, and, yes, worrying about them "liking" you and "having fun" at your house. Kids need you to be a parent, not a pal.

30.

Make your kids' transitions consistent and stress-free.

Even when it's become a regular routine, switching houses or leaving one parent to be with the other can be stressful for kids. You may notice behavior changes or issues in the hours before and after these transitions. Living in two places and/or going back and forth between parents can be tough. Cut them some slack until they adjust to their routine. Don't get angry when items are forgotten.

Follow these tips for smooth transitions:

- Have their belongings packed and ready to go in advance (or if they're older, give them reminders). (See Children's Transition-Day Checklist, appendix F.)
- Be relaxed and helpful at transition time.
- Avoid any negative interaction with your ex.
- If you can't get along with your ex during transitions, make an alternate plan (for example, have kids say their good-byes in the car at dropoff time.)

31.

Watch your kids for emotional and behavioral red flags.

With kids, who often are unable to express their feelings logically or with words, you sometimes need to be a detective along with being a parent. Watch for these clues. Your child may need to see a professional if you notice one or more of these signs:

- Significant anxiety
- Significant depression
- Persistent defiance and/or negative behavior
- Problems with peers
- Eating less or eating more
- Low energy
- Academic decline
- Suicidal talk or attempt
- Easily angered
- Biting nails
- Bedwetting
- Psychosomatic symptoms (hypochondria)
- Headaches
- Sleep problems
- Pulling out hair or eyelashes (or any self mutilation, such as unexplained cuts or abrasions)

32.
Don't burn bridges; the kids need them.

Continue whatever connections you can to your ex's side of the family. Try to stay on good terms so the children can have an ongoing relationship with their grandparents, aunts, uncles, cousins, etc. Not only are these people important relations of your kids, your path will likely continue to cross with theirs—at graduations, weddings, etc.—for a long time to come. Make the effort, reach out even if they don't; you'll be rewarded in the long run.

33.

Don't start dating before you're ready.

Five signs you're not ready to date:

1. **It's been less than a year.** We recommend you not start dating seriously for at least a year after you separate. You need to find yourself again and discover what kind of person and relationship is right for you. A casual date to get your feet wet may be fine, depending on your ability to keep it light. If you jump into dating too soon, you're likely to have a "rebound" relationship that crashes and burns.

2. **You think about your ex or your ex comes up in conversation every day.** If you aren't 100 percent sure whether this is the case, ask your most brutally honest friends.

3. **You feel uncomfortable or incomplete not being part of a couple.** A successful relationship involves two people who are comfortable and content on their own, who want to be together but don't need to be.

4. **When you talk about your divorce or your ex, your anger still comes through loud and clear.** Before starting something new with someone else, you need to be past the anger stage and have reached acceptance.

5. **You still blame your ex entirely and don't understand how you contributed to the problems in your marriage.** It's very important to find and own your part in the breakdown of your marriage so that you don't make the same mistakes in the future.

34.

Don't introduce your kids too soon to a new significant other.

Let's face it: sometimes we aren't thinking clearly when we're in the throes of a new relationship. Be aware of this and protect your children. Only introduce your kids to a significant other when you *know* that person will be in your life long-term. A revolving door of romances just means more loss for your kids.

Note: If you can, make an agreement with your ex on a time frame for introducing significant others to the kids. Also, you may want to agree to tell each other first. Again, this kind of respectful and mature behavior is great for your children to see.

35.

Prep for the holidays when you'll be alone.

Be proactive and make fun plans for the holidays. Whether it's Valentine's Day, Christmas, Thanksgiving, Easter, etc., think outside the box and start new traditions. Be silly, indulgent, or extravagant. Here are some ideas to get your wheels turning:

- Pamper yourself. Splurge on something you wouldn't normally do for yourself—get a massage or a whole day at a spa, buy something special at your favorite store, or simply take a long, indulgent bubble bath.

- Throw a party. Invite all your single friends (and perhaps tell them to bring a friend or two of the opposite sex). This is a great way to expand your network.
- Plan a fun night out with friends. Treat yourself to a great show or even just a movie. When was the last time you went dancing?
- If you have kids, focus the occasion on them. Spoil them with a special dinner, bake something fun for dessert, and watch a funny movie.
- If your ex will have the kids, take a fun trip or visit family or friends.

36.

Going back to work can be a positive change.

If you haven't been working outside the home and need to get a job now, don't fret about how it might affect your kids. They'll see you earning money, modeling a good work ethic, managing your time, and showing competence. They'll be fine.

37.
You will get through this.

This too shall pass. Your divorce will be part of your past. You've been given a fresh start, and a wonderful, new life lies ahead of you now. Just remember, the choices you make today will become a chapter in your life story. Choose and act with integrity and grace. When you look back on this time, you want to be proud of how you handled it.

Now you have the tools and inspiration to start over smart.

Appendixes

For free access to downloads of the forms and lists on the following pages, visit: www.StartOverSmartDivorceAdvisors.com.

Appendix A

Budget Form

Fill out two budget forms, one for your current (pre-separation) expenses, and one for your projected post-separation expenses. *List all expenses as monthly.* To calculate monthly amounts, divide annual expenses by 12 and multiply weekly expenses by 4.33 (the average number of weeks in a month).

A) Housing

(If you own more than one residence, create separate lists for each.)

Mortgage payment (first mortgage)	_____
Home equity loan (second mortgage)	_____
Condominium/cooperative charges	_____
Taxes, if paid separately from mortgage	_____
Homeowners insurance (if paid separately)	_____
Rent	_____
Parking (where you live)	_____
TOTAL (A)	_____

B) Utilities

(If you own more than one residence, create separate lists for each.)

1. Gas/electric _____
2. Home phone _____
3. Cell phone _____

4. Cable TV/satellite   _____

5. DSL line   _____

6. Internet service   _____

7. Security/alarm   _____

8. Pest control (if monthly)   _____

9. Heating oil/propane   _____

10. Garbage removal   _____

11. Water/sewer   _____

12. Gardening/mowing/sprinkler   _____

13. Pool   _____

14. Snow plow   _____

15. Firewood   _____

16. Other (indicate)   _____

TOTAL (B)   _____

Fixed Monthly Housing Expenses (A + B)   _____

C) Household maintenance

(If you own more than one residence, create separate lists for each.)

1. Ongoing repairs (carpenter, electrician, plumbers, etc.)   _____

2. Replacement of furniture, linens, etc. (not new purchases)   _____

3. Maintenance of appliances (service contracts)   _____

4. Replacement of appliances (heating, a/c, TVs, etc.)   _____

5. Painting (inside and outside, calculated monthly amount)   _____

6. Pest control (if not included above as monthly cost   _____

7. House cleaning (regular ongoing service)   _____

8. Heavy-duty periodic cleaning (i.e., window washing)   _____

9. Carpet and furniture cleaning   _____

10. Maintenance of furnace/chimney   _____

               TOTAL (C)   _____

D) Food

1. Supermarket (food and non-food items)   _____

2. Delivery/"takeout"   _____

3. Extra cost for holiday meals   _____

4. Pet food   _____

               TOTAL (D)   _____

E) Clothing

1. Self   _____

2. Outside laundry service   _____

3. Dry cleaning   _____

               TOTAL (E)   _____

F) Automobiles (list information for each automobile separately)

Year: _____

Make   _____

Lease?   _____

Payments end   _____

1. Monthly payments   _____
2. Gas   _____
3. Maintenance and repairs   _____
4. Insurance   _____
5. Registration fees, taxes, road service (AAA)   _____
6. Garage parking (if extra expense)   _____
7. Tolls/EZ pass, tickets, car wash   _____

TOTAL (F)   _____

G) Health plan/services

1. Insurance premium
    (may be different going forward)   _____
2. Coinsurance cost
    (# of monthly visits x co-pay)   _____
3. Unreimbursed or uncovered medical   _____
4. Unreimbursed dental   _____
5. Unreimbursed orthodontics; balance owed   _____
6. Optical (exam plus costs of glasses or contacts)   _____
7. Medicine/drugs (# prescriptions x copayment)   _____
8. Nonprescription medicines,
    if not already included   _____
9. Psychotherapy (after reimbursement)   _____
10.   Other (indicate)   _____

TOTAL (G)   _____

H) Insurance (non-health) and professional services

1. Life insurance (through employment)   _____

2. Life insurance: face amount
   $_____ and monthly cost   _____

3. Disability—indicate benefit
   $_____ and monthly cost   _____

4. Umbrella policy (separate and in
   addition to homeowners)   _____

5. Long-term care insurance   _____

6. Accountant, financial planner, attorney, etc. _____

7. Other (indicate)   _____

                              TOTAL (H)   _____

I) Loans and credit card payments

1. Student loans: total owed
   $_____ and monthly payments   _____

2. Credit cards:

   AmEx   _____

   MCard   _____

   Visa   _____

   Discover   _____

   Dept. Store   _____

   Other   _____

3. Overdraft checking   _____

4. Personal loan   _____

5. Other (indicate)   _____

                              TOTAL (I)   _____

J) Education (list each person separately)

For: _____

1. Private school (net after scholarships)

    Tuition   _____

    Additional contribution   _____

    Transportation   _____

    Books and supplies   _____

    Uniforms   _____

    Lunch (if paid annually)   _____

    Other (indicate)   _____

For: _____

2. College (net after scholarships)

    Tuition   _____

    Room and board   _____

    Books and supplies   _____

    Fees   _____

    Transportation   _____

    Allowance   _____

    Other (indicate)   _____

                                  TOTAL (J)   _____

K) Direct child expenses

1. Child-care person—salary, fees, taxes, etc.   _____

2. Babysitter in addition to above   _____

3. Day care/nursery school   _____

4. After-school costs (include holiday periods)   _____

5. Summer camp and related expenses   _____

6. Music and other lessons　　　　　　＿＿＿＿＿＿＿

7. Tutoring　　　　　　＿＿＿＿＿＿＿

8. Religious instruction　　　　　　＿＿＿＿＿＿＿

9. Sports teams and equipment　　　　　　＿＿＿＿＿＿＿

10. Toys, games, etc.　　　　　　＿＿＿＿＿＿＿

11. Computer hardware and software　　　　　　＿＿＿＿＿＿＿

12. School lunches/snacks　　　　　　＿＿＿＿＿＿＿

13. School extras (supplies, trips, etc.)　　　　　　＿＿＿＿＿＿＿

14. Trips taken without parents　　　　　　＿＿＿＿＿＿＿

15. Gifts for children's friends (birthdays, etc.)　　　　　　＿＿＿＿＿＿＿

16. Cell phone (phone and monthly coverage)　　　　　　＿＿＿＿＿＿＿

17. Haircuts and other personal care　　　　　　＿＿＿＿＿＿＿

18. Allowance　　　　　　＿＿＿＿＿＿＿

19. Birthday parties and other celebrations　　　　　　＿＿＿＿＿＿＿

20. Teacher gifts　　　　　　＿＿＿＿＿＿＿

21. Dental/orthodontics　　　　　　＿＿＿＿＿＿＿

22. Car (car and gas)　　　　　　＿＿＿＿＿＿＿

23. Clothes　　　　　　＿＿＿＿＿＿＿

24. Cosmetics/toiletries　　　　　　＿＿＿＿＿＿＿

25. Other (indicate)　　　　　　＿＿＿＿＿＿＿

TOTAL (K)　　＿＿＿＿＿＿＿

L) Recreation/entertainment/personal care (separate amounts for self and children)

Self:

1. Eating out　　　　　　＿＿＿＿＿＿＿

2. Movies　　　　　　＿＿＿＿＿＿＿

3. Theater and concerts　　　　　　＿＿＿＿＿＿＿

4. Spectator sports   _____

5. Weekend vacations   _____

6. Annual vacations (winter, spring, summer)   _____

7. Hobbies   _____

8. Purchase of books, CDs, DVDs, iTunes, etc.   _____

9. Gym   _____

10. Personal trainer   _____

11. Hair salon/barber   _____

12. Manicure/pedicure   _____

13. Cosmetics/toiletries   _____

14. Other (indicate)   _____

Children:

1. Eating out   _____

2. Movies   _____

3. Theater and concerts   _____

4. Spectator sports   _____

5. Weekend vacations   _____

6. Annual vacations (winter, spring, summer)   _____

7. Hobbies   _____

8. Purchase of books, CDs, DVDs, iTunes, etc.   _____

9. Gym   _____

10. Personal trainer   _____

11. Hair salon/barber   _____

12. Manicure/pedicure   _____

13. Cosmetics/toiletries   _____

14. Other (indicate)   _____

                        TOTAL (L)   _____

M) Miscellaneous

1. Magazine, newspaper, etc. (subscriptions plus daily   _____

2. Museum memberships   _____

3. Union and organization dues   _____

4. Gifts (holidays, birthdays, etc.)   _____

5. Holiday expenses (decorations, tips, etc.)   _____

6. Pet expenses (if not already included)   _____

7. Church or synagogue dues   _____

8. Charitable contributions   _____

9. Car service, taxi cabs   _____

10. Transportation and commuter costs (e.g., Metrocard)   _____

11. Spending money (lunch, snacks, cigarettes, etc.)   _____

12. Alimony/maintenance/child support (from prior marriage)   _____

13. Savings contributions (college, 401(k), etc.)   _____

14. Country clubs   _____

15. Office/computer supplies for the home   _____

16. Postage   _____

TOTAL (M)   _____

TOTAL EXPENSES: (sum of A through M) $_____

Get free access to a downloadable PDF of this form at www.StartOverSmartDivorceAdvisors.com.

Appendix B

Net Income Sheet

Collect your last three years' W2s and tax returns, and fill out this form for the past year.

Monthly Income

1. Gross salary/wages _____
2. Bonus, commissions, fringe benefits (e.g., a company car) _____
3. Partnerships, royalties _____
4. Sale of assets _____
5. Dividends and interest _____
6. Real estate (income only) _____
7. Award, prizes, and grants _____
8. Child support _____
9. Maintenance/alimony _____
10. Unemployment _____
11. Disability income _____
12. Worker's comp _____
13. Other income _____

Monthly Deductions

a. Social security _____
b. State/federal tax _____

c. Other payroll tax _____

d. Medicare _____

e. Other deductions _____

Total Net Income (Income - Deductions) = _____

Get free access to a downloadable PDF of this form at www.StartOverSmartDivorceAdvisors.com.

Appendix C

Assets and Liabilities List

Assets

1. Checking accounts
2. Savings accounts (including CDs and money market accounts)
3. Stocks and bonds
4. Mutual funds and investments accounts
5. Life insurance policies
6. Real estate (rentals, second homes, land, etc.)
7. IRAs, 401(k)s, pensions, profit sharing, deferred compensation, trusts, etc.
8. Jewelry, furs, art, antiques, precious objects, gold and precious metals (total market value)
9. Other assets (money owed to you, tax shelter investments, collections, judgments, causes of action, patents, trademarks, copyrights, and any other assets not listed above, at market value)

Liabilities

1. Mortgages
2. Car loans
3. Installment accounts (credit cards, bank loans, department stores, etc.)

4. Back taxes owed
5. Other liabilities (including loans on life insurance policies)

Get free access to a downloadable PDF of this form at www.StartOverSmartDivorceAdvisors.com.

Appendix D

Sample Move-Out Agreement

This is an informal and generic agreement form. Ask an attorney to review this and any documents before signing.

This agreement confirms that I will move out of our home at _____ (address) on _____ (date) so that we can have our own space in which to work toward a resolution of our marital problems.

We agree:

My leaving will not constitute "abandonment" and that I will retain any and all rights I have to our house, our marital assets, and our children.

I can move back into the house at any time, during this interim period, as long as I give you ample notice.

Any amount of money transferred from one of us to the other during this interim period, whether as a distribution of our assets, spousal support, or child support, will not be used as evidence or referred to in any court proceedings for any purpose, including to show that either of us can pay such amounts or that either of us needs or deserves such amounts.

Any interim arrangement we make regarding the parenting of our children will not be used as evidence or referred to in any court proceedings for any purpose, including to show what is in the children's best interests or to show what arrangements are workable or appropriate for our family.

Signed on _____ (date)

_____ (spouse staying in house)

_____ (spouse moving out of house)

Get free access to a downloadable PDF of this form at
www.StartOverSmartDivorceAdvisors.com.

Appendix E

Children's Bill of Rights

This list of rights is appropriate to share with your children ages nine and older (but you know your kids best; use your own judgment).

As a child of divorced parents, the adults in your life need to respect your rights. If you feel your parents aren't respecting all the rights below, it's important to talk to them or another adult (a grandparent, aunt or uncle, counselor, pediatrician, teacher, etc.).

My rights as a child of divorced parents include:

1. The right to love both my parents without guilt or interference from the other parent;
2. The right not to hear either parent say anything bad about the other;
3. The right to be a child, left out of adult worries and conflicts;
4. The right to ask questions and have them answered respectfully, with age-appropriate detail, without blaming or belittling anyone;
5. The right to regular contact with both parents and other family members;
6. The right not to be questioned about the other parent or his or her household;
7. The right to have and display photos of both parents;
8. The right to live in relaxed, secure environments with both parents;
9. The right not to be asked to choose sides or to be put in situations where I have to choose;
10. The right to refuse to be a messenger and deliver messages, notes, documents, etc., from one parent to the other;

11. The right to be protected from overhearing arguments, angry words, or adult issues;
12. The right to talk to another adult (therapist, guidance counselor, trusted friend) about my concerns;
13. The right to enjoy my time with each parent;
14. The right to speak honestly and express my true feelings without feeling guilty;
15. The right to communicate with both parents as often as needed;
16. The right to celebrate special events with both parents; and
17. The right to see my parents engage in healthy relationships and behaviors.

Get free access to a downloadable PDF of this form at www.StartOverSmartDivorceAdvisors.com.

Appendix F

Children's Transition-Day Checklist

Use this list or create your own. It can be hard on kids when they leave things they need at their other house, so do everything you can to help them stay organized and remember things they want to take with them. Use checklists like this and create routines such as putting "to go" items by the front door the night before transition day.

Security blanket or stuffed animal (for younger children)

Sports equipment/jerseys/uniform (list items, e.g., hat, mitt, cup, mouth guard, etc.)

Dressy or special clothing or items for an upcoming event (concert at school, party, church, etc.)

Reading book

Schoolbooks/supplies

Wax, rubber bands, cleaning tools, etc., for braces

Retainer

Eyeglasses/sunglasses

Prescriptions

Electronics (cell phones, e-readers, tablets, laptops, including chargers)

Musical instruments

Sneakers/cleats/dress shoes for an upcoming event or game

Other: _____

_____

_____

_____

Get free access to a downloadable PDF of this form at
www.StartOverSmartDivorceAdvisors.com.

Appendix G

Holidays and Vacations Scheduling Chart

—A common convention is to assign even years to one parent and odd years to the other parent for the major holidays.

—Make caveats/arrangements for overlapping holidays (e.g., if Christmas or Passover falls during winter break, or if a birthday falls on a holiday or during a break, how will the scheduling be handled?).

—Some parents agree to allow the children to spend all Monday holidays with whichever parent they are with for that weekend rather than divvy up the Monday holidays.

Holiday	Which parent has child(ren)
New Year's Eve	
New Year's Day	
Martin Luther King Day	
President's Day	
Passover first night	
Passover second night	
Good Friday	
Easter Sunday	
Mother's Day	
Memorial Day	
Father's Day	

July Fourth	
Labor Day	
Rosh Hashanah first day	
Rosh Hashanah second day	
Yom Kippur	
Columbus Day	
Halloween	
Election Day	
Veterans Day	
Thanksgiving Day	
Chanukah first night	
Christmas Eve	
Christmas Day	
Child's birthday	
Mother's birthday	
Father's birthday	
School breaks	
Winter break	
Spring break	
Summer break	

Get free access to a downloadable PDF of this form at
www.StartOverSmartDivorceAdvisors.com.

Appendix H

Affidavit of Parental Consent for Travel

(A minor child traveling without both birth parents)

I, _____ (name) _____ (relation) of said minor child, do hereby authorize _____ (name) _____ (relation) of said minor child to travel as a guardian of _____ (minor child's name), age: _____, to the following countries without me:

_____

_____

_____

_____

From: Day: _____ /Month: _____ /Year: _____

To: Day: _____ /Month: _____ /Year: _____

I [ ] AUTHORIZE   [ ] DO NOT AUTHORIZE

the above-named person to make medical treatment decisions for the minor child listed above if needed. If not, we have provided emergency contact information below:

Name: _____

Address: _____

City/State/Zip: _____

Home Phone: (_____) _____

Work Phone: (_____) _____

Alternate Name and Phone:_____

_____

_____

Signature: _____

(Signature of non-traveling birth parent(s) to be signed in front of a notary public only)

Subscribed and sworn to before me this _____ day of _____, 20_____

Signature of notary public: _____

Get free access to a downloadable PDF of this form at www.StartOverSmartDivorceAdvisors.com.

Notes

Notes

Notes

Notes

Notes

Important Contacts

Name	Phone and Email
Divorce advisor/coach	
Lawyer	
Mediator	
Financial planner	
Accountant	
Therapist	
Children's therapist	
Parenting expert	
Massage therapist	
Babysitter	
Friends & family	
Clergy	
Support group	
Gym	
Other	

Made in the USA
San Bernardino, CA
26 January 2015